Luke House is a Licensed Clinical Professional Counselor (Conditional) with a private practice in Windham, Maine, and a Gold Star Brother after the death of his younger brother, Sgt. Joel House, who died while serving in Iraq in 2007. Since Joel's death, Luke has been involved with the founding and operation of *House in the Woods,* a Maine non-profit started by his father, that brings veterans and their family members on healing retreats in rural Maine.

In his practice, Luke works with a variety of individuals including the general public, veterans and first responders, and incarcerated individuals. A niche area for Luke is **"Grief** and **Loss",** as he incorporates his personal experience, graduate education, and many hours of additional training on helping people integrate grief and loss into positive growth in their lives.

Guerrilla Grief: The Men's Grief Manual is an accumulation of Luke's personal and professional experience in which he seeks to guide men through their unique grief and loss journey so that they grow and find purpose in their lives after loss.

TABLE OF CONTENTS

GUERRILLA GRIEF

THE MEN'S

Grief Manual

WIN THE WAR FOR YOUR HEART

BY LUKE HOUSE LCPC-C

CHAPTER 1

The current state of affairs can be described as a **"crisis,"** though this may not be a surprise to most people. Every day, when we turn on the news, we hear about one crisis or another. However, there is a very real crisis that is not getting the attention it deserves. It's a crisis that pervades everything around us and yet goes largely unnoticed. If you're reading this, then chances are you already know something about this crisis, which I have experienced firsthand. It nearly destroyed me once, but it also provided me with the key to changing my world in every positive way. Although the last few years have highlighted this issue due to the COVID-19 pandemic, it is something that has always been a part of the human experience, *particularly for men.*

Men experience grief in a way that is often overlooked. It is not just sadness, but the devastating loss of loved ones, identity, culture, heritage, and purpose. The issue that I observe here is that men are ashamed to admit that they're grieving, causing them to suffer silently. This makes it challenging because grief is often not even considered a possibility for a man or group of men who may be struggling, acting out in confrontation or confusion, unable to produce, or unable to live fulfilling lives of purpose. While death is a significant part of grief, it's not the only one. Divorce, betrayal, job loss, career loss, housing loss, political shifts, and ideological confusion are all losses that men commonly experience.

My own experiences and research about grief have shown me that grief is a powerful force that does not discriminate nor ask for permission to enter anyone's life. Grief does not need to be acknowledged to take effect and can hold a firm grip on someone's life if left unacknowledged. Sometimes, grief remains stuck and builds up behind a dam of shame, unawareness, and an inability to push through it.

Picture a massive hydroelectric dam, an engineering marvel that transforms the relentless flow of water into electricity, illuminating homes and energizing entire cities. When this dam operates smoothly, the results are nothing short of astonishing. It's a testament to how nature's force, tamed and controlled, can benefit humanity, showcasing the beauty of collaboration between man and nature.

But let's venture into another scenario, one all too familiar in the face of natural disasters like hurricanes or earthquakes. This same dam reaches its capacity, struggling to contain the mounting water pressure. As it weakens, the inevitable happens: the dam begins to crumble, and eventually, it erupts. The consequences are catastrophic. What was once a source of power now becomes an agent of destruction. The initial impact is devastating. As the unchecked force of water wreaks havoc, buildings crumble, lives are lost, roads vanish, and chaos reigns.

In many ways, grief mirrors this analogy, particularly for men. When we refuse to acknowledge or accept our grief for what it is, we deny it the opportunity to flow in a healthy manner. We bottle it up, pretend it doesn't exist, and continue with our lives as if avoidance could somehow make it vanish. But it doesn't disappear; instead, it persists. Signs may surface after weeks, months, or even years, and they often manifest in unexpected ways. Personally, I've experienced what I'd call "**Anger Grieving**," a common phenomenon among men. We carry the pain silently, and it seeps out as anger directed toward loved ones, colleagues, strangers, or the world at large. We're hurting, yet expressing this hurt openly seems somehow unacceptable. Sometimes, this anger simmers slowly, and other times, the dam bursts! The aftermath of such an explosion is a painful tapestry of regret, missed opportunities, and self-inflicted wounds.

But there's a flip side to this covert struggle—a side that's equally powerful as the controlled release of a well-maintained dam, providing boundless energy to the world around it. When we confront and embrace our grief, we unlock the potential for transformation beyond our wildest expectations. We tap into the deep well of emotions—love, loss, sadness, confusion, meaning, and hope—that grief encompasses. A community influenced by men who acknowledge and integrate their grief thrives and flourishes. Their positive impact reverberates throughout society, touching men, women, children, workplaces, community organizations, charities, and beyond.

In this context, embracing and integrating grief isn't just a personal journey; it's a transformative force that can elevate entire communities and societies. One of the greatest examples I have of this, a man in grief and him using that grief to create, is the story of *House in the Woods*. I will refer to *House in the Woods* throughout the manual.

The genesis of *House in the Woods* is a testament to the power of purpose and resilience, born out of the most profound loss. It was an idea sparked by a divine moment, etched into the heart of my father, Paul House, not long after my brother Joel's tragic death while serving in the U.S. Army in Iraq. We stood together at a memorial in Fort Hood, Texas, honoring Joel and the 17 other brave soldiers from his unit who had fallen in June 2007. There, we found solace in the home of a colonel and major, a husband and wife who had known Joel through their church and had often welcomed him into their lives. They described him as the kind of man they'd wish their daughter to marry.

My father vividly recalls that moment, tears streaming down his face, as he felt God's voice speaking to him—a divine calling. The message was clear:

"You're going to build a place in Maine for soldiers and their families to come together and heal amid the serenity of the Maine woods."

And so, propelled by the pain of my brother's loss, my father embarked on the journey to create.

In my work as a counselor, I find that it is helpful to break healing of all types into manageable and easily identified segments. As a very practical and straightforward approach to *Guerilla Grief*, I developed the **PPRESS** acronym, which is the meat and potatoes of this grief manual. **PPRRESS** —a template I employ in *Guerilla Grief* seeks to explore the "Purpose," "Physical," "Resilience," "Remembrance," "Emotion," "Social," and "Spiritual" aspects of healing. I also find that "simplicity" is most effective in working through substantial loss. As I developed the material for this manual, "simplicity" and "effectiveness" were my main objectives. I will even put a disclaimer here that I truly feel much of this material is obvious and I hope that it is. I say this because I believe we often intuitively know what we need to do to heal but we don't allow our intuition to inform our path. I seek to affirm your intuition and to tap into your natural instincts to heal.

Each chapter in the main body of this grief manual is an element of **PPRRESS** that we will explore, give actionable steps to employ, and anecdotes from my personal experience where **PPRRESS** has been utilized as a means for integrating grief. The acronym **PPRRESS** also serves as a reminder to press forward, even when things feel challenging, hopeless, or downright impossible.

PPRRESS is meant to be referred to and assessed daily as a straightforward way of keeping track of and maintaining progress. I prefer to use a small Likert scale of 1-5 to rate each of the categories "Purpose," "Physical well-being," "Resilience," "Remembrance," "Social," and "Spiritual." A rating of "1" denotes that there is much room for improvement. It's okay to rate a "1" as long as you are honest. This allows awareness of where to double your efforts. A "5" would indicate that you are doing very well overall in a category. A "5" does not mean perfection but that you have a relatively solid hold on the category. The numbers between 1 and 5 acknowledge that there is room for improvement.

As a long-time martial arts enthusiast, I've always found wisdom in the teachings of Sun Tzu. Among his many valuable insights, Sun Tzu offered a strategic and encompassing approach to guerrilla warfare—a tactic born from the unconventional, a means to harass and overcome larger forces through non-traditional means and participants. This approach played a crucial role in the American Revolution, where seemingly insurmountable odds were defied. One of my all-time favorite films, "*The Patriot*," vividly portrays the effectiveness of guerrilla warfare in the face of overwhelming adversity.

As I delved into Sun Tzu's principles and explored the unconventional realm of guerrilla warfare, I couldn't help but draw parallels to grief and loss. Much like guerrilla warfare, grief defies convention and resists straightforward solutions. It's messy and confusing and there's no one-size-fits-all approach, regardless of what anyone claims. Hence, the term "*Guerrilla Grief*" resonates—it signifies the need to employ any means necessary to confront loss in a way that integrates it into our lives, fostering *healing*, *change*, and *purpose*.

The subtitle, "*The Men's Grief Manual*," underscores the instructional aspect of my work—a guide to address crucial areas when navigating the complexities of grief. In the realm of healing professions, learning from someone with firsthand experience is often most beneficial. In this grief manual, I'll draw extensively from my personal journey through grief and loss, with a particular focus on the profound impact of my baby brother Sgt. Joel House's combat death, who tragically lost his life in Iraq on June 23, 2007. I'll share how I've implemented these healing strategies, both successfully and otherwise, shedding light on the transformative power they hold when employed effectively.

I will also incorporate stories from *House in the Woods* which is a 501 C3 Nonprofit started with the original idea from my father after my brother was killed in the war. A bit of a timeline of *House in the Woods* will serve well here.

My dad was a logger, as that is one of the main vocations in rural Maine. As kids, my brother, sister, and I would see him leave the house early in all of the elements, extreme heat, cold, rain, and snow, to cut wood with his skidders (log hauling machines) or his draft horses. The work is hard and often thankless, sometimes feast or famine. As an avid hunter and outdoorsman, my dad decided to obtain his Maine Guides license so that he could bring sports on hunting trips into the Maine woods. My brother, dad, and I also hunted and fished together which served as a time for bonding and to do the things that we love in nature. To say that the outdoors is a part of our life would be an understatement. With the last name of "House," *House in the Woods* was the only logical name for his guide service.

Early on, my parents, Paul and Deanna, started by utilizing donated camp spaces and the support of guide outfits that hosted veterans on outdoor retreats. Despite numerous setbacks and growing pains, the unwavering purpose led the way. Today, *House in the Woods* has touched the lives of thousands of veterans from across the nation, offering them a haven for healing.

Ultimately, the purpose found a way to manifest as a $3.5 million, ADA-accessible retreat building, affectionately known as "*the lodge*." This remarkable structure features an ADA elevator, a gourmet kitchen, and accommodations for over 18 veterans at a time. It's not about boasting; it's a testament to the significance of finding a purpose in the aftermath of a loss, utilizing that loss as fuel, and persevering through every step in between.

***What qualifies me to write about men's grief?*

It's a question I've often pondered, and it's a question you might be asking too. The simplest answer is this: I'm a man who has walked the path of grief in various ways throughout my life. I've navigated grief both in what some might call the "hard way" and the "healthy way." The key distinction I've found between the two is a single word: "acknowledgment."

When I've acknowledged my losses, I've opened myself up to seek help and support. In that acknowledgment, I've come to accept that this is not business as usual. Grief is a season of life where everything feels different. We experience emotions we've never felt before, we act in ways that might not make sense to others, and we discover new paths forward that we never imagined.

Later in my journey, I serendipitously became a licensed clinical professional counselor. Looking back, it all makes sense now. My losses, scattered across the chapters of my life, ultimately led me to this profession, though I could have never planned such a path. Through counseling, I've found my true calling. As a man with a history of acknowledged grief experiences, I possess a profound passion for helping others navigate loss in a meaningful and growth-enhancing way.

It's interesting to note that my counseling licensure mandates over 40 hours of continuing education, spanning various theories and modalities. However, I've chosen to dedicate a disproportionate amount of my time to studying "grief and loss" specifically. I often tell my clients, as an ice-breaker, that I'm passionate about grief. It sometimes elicits a chuckle, but it's the truth. "Grief" is a subject that even seasoned practitioners sometimes avoid. It's raw, it brings forth the most genuine emotions and experiences, and it's undeniably uncomfortable. Bearing witness to someone's pain requires a deep presence.

In my relatively short time as a counselor, I've sat with many men and women who have endured what may seem like insurmountable losses. These include suicide, the loss of children, spouses, and siblings, devastating divorces, career setbacks, and more. I consider myself truly blessed every time someone trusts me with their most vulnerable life experiences.

As you read my words, I encourage you to view my life experiences, education, professional journey, and humanity not as credentials that make me an authority on your grief but as an individual genuinely interested in guiding and supporting you. My aim is to contribute to a world where growth and healing are central, helping each of us move forward on our unique paths through grief.**

I distinctly remember the moment when I learned that my brother Joel had been killed on June 23rd, 2007. This day marked a turning point in my life that I will never forget. At the time, I was living in Seattle, Washington, having moved there from Florida after a difficult break-up. I was pursuing a career in executive protection and had taken up a job with a moving company. On that fateful day, I heard a news story on NPR about four US soldiers and an Iraqi interpreter who were killed by a roadside bomb in Taji, Iraq. My brother's deployment was in that area, and so the news immediately caught my attention. I breathed a sigh of relief when the story ended without any names given, but I was still apprehensive.

Later that day, my father called and asked me where I was and if I was with anyone. I knew by his voice that something terrible had happened, and I immediately assumed that my grandmother had passed away. That would have been bad enough, but the next words that he spoke shook me to my core.

"Joel's been killed. Two men from the military just left the house."

My entire world collapsed at that moment, and I was unable to make sense of anything. Joel had been in a convoy in which his Humvee drove on top of an improvised explosive device. When the convoy stopped the IED was remotely detonated killing Joel, Lt. Matthew Riordon, Specialist Jimmy Malone, CPL Derrick Calhoun, and an Iraq interpreter called " Eagle" I called my roommate and good friend, Matt, who was at work and also the only friend that I had in Seattle. When I told him that my brother had been killed in Iraq, he immediately took the day off. I felt as though I was falling off a building with no end in sight. I was in shock and too confused to cry. It was only later that it all started to sink in.

While most people think of grief as being related only to death, it can also be caused by the experience of loss in other domains of life. This is a common theme among my therapy clients, and I often find that they are experiencing grief without even realizing it.

As I began to hone in on a niche area, I found that *"**grief work**"* was one crucial area that I am incredibly passionate about. As I began to work with clients in grief due to the death of a loved one, I began to notice very similar themes to those clients who had experienced loss other than death. For example, a male client going through a recent and unexpected divorce had turned his whole world upside down. My training and education taught me that grief was not unique to death. However, my clients began to show me how true this is in living color.

I began to utilize grief as a framework to help my clients navigate any substantial loss in their lives. One client had unexpectedly ended a law enforcement career of more than 25 years. He had mixed feelings and a lot of anger toward ending this career. I will never forget the day we began to use grief to let go of the career loss and move on.

"It just makes sense," he said.

We routinely returned to the grief framework, and he found it applicable to many areas of his life. As I worked with clients in this capacity, my understanding of the various losses in my own life also began to make much more sense. At age four, I was diagnosed with a tumor called an *"optic nerve glioma."* This tumor was benign but would continue to grow indefinitely and could cause many issues. My parents decided to have it removed.

The doctors assured them with 100 percent certainty that my optic nerve would be severed and I would be blind in my left eye. At one appointment, my father questioned the doctor and begged him to replace his eye with mine. The doctor told him that an eye transplant was impossible; there was no alternative. The surgery ensued; as predicted, I was blind in one eye upon waking. I don't remember feeling any different at this time. Life went on as usual, and I was a relatively normal child.

It wasn't until I began to attempt sports as an older child that it became apparent that the eye loss had a substantial impact on my depth perception and coordination. I tried all sports, and maybe I was not a natural athlete, but the eye thing made it very hard. I rarely connected with a ball at bat.

Early Loss

Loss is a universal experience that we encounter at different times and in various ways throughout our lives. Some losses occur early on and are not immediately comprehensible. I can vividly recall my first encounter with "death" when I was around three years old. My great-grandfather had left a lasting impression on me despite the ongoing debate about the age at which our earliest long-term memories form. I can still recall visiting the home he shared with my great-grandmother.

In retrospect, it becomes clear that he was in a hospital bed situated in the living room. He had cancer and was spending his final days at home, surrounded by loved ones. At that age, I was unaware of his illness and impending death; the concept of death had not yet taken shape in my mind. What remains vivid in my memory is the delightful experience of him sharing his tasty nutritional drinks with me. Even to this day, I find myself enjoying and craving the taste of the vanilla *Ensure*, which serves as my earliest memory of a distinct flavor. I also hold fond recollections of the scent of his tobacco pipe as he would smoke and engage in conversations from his leather chair.

One day, upon visiting, I discovered my great-grandfather's absence. I inquired about his whereabouts, asking my grandmother, "*Where is Grampie Mickey?*" She responded, "*He's not here; he's in heaven.*" I found this notion amusing and laughed. I persisted, seeking a more tangible answer, asking, "*No, where is he really!?*" It's difficult to recall the exact words exchanged, but the interaction remains crystal clear in my mind. I spent hours inquiring in various ways, perplexed by my grandmother's refusal to disclose his location. I don't remember the outcome of that day, only that my childhood continued relatively unchanged.

Among my early memories, this experience stands out alongside a few others from around the same age. I can recall accompanying my father on bird hunts, observing him with a shotgun in hand. We would venture near my grandparents' farm, where my father had grown up with his fourteen siblings and numerous relatives. Cows, horses, and chickens still roamed the property during my early years. I distinctly remember clutching my father's hand as we strolled through the apple orchard adjacent to the horse pasture. *"Daddy, why is the horse climbing the tree?"* I exclaimed. Suddenly and swiftly, my father grabbed my hand, and we ran. It turned out that what I mistook for a tree-climbing horse was actually a bear cub, with its mother nearby, watchful and protective. One should never come between a mother bear and her cubs. My father, being aware of this, did not trust that his old single-shot 12-gauge shotgun loaded with birdshot would suffice if the mother bear felt threatened.

So, what does this little anecdote have to do with loss? Quite a lot, actually. Allow me to explain. Just as I lacked the understanding of what my great-grandfather's death truly meant, I also had no frame of reference for comprehending a bear in the wild. Prior to that moment, my encounters with bears had been limited to stuffed animals, books, and photographs. I had seen cows, pigs, chickens, and horses before, but never a bear. In choosing the horse as the most likely candidate for an animal climbing a tree, I based my assumption on proximity and recent visual exposure. All the context my developing mind could provide suggested that the creature I observed must be a horse ascending the tree.

Erik Erikson often employs the concept of "Staging" to describe the progression of psychosocial development. According to his theory, our understanding and perception of the world are influenced by our past experiences and the knowledge we have acquired thus far. Erikson's theory outlines eight stages that occur across the lifespan, including "trust vs. mistrust," "autonomy vs. shame and doubt," "initiative vs. guilt," "industry vs. inferiority," "identity vs. role confusion," "intimacy vs. isolation," "generativity vs. stagnation," and "integrity vs. despair." However, it's important to note that grief, too, can be understood in stages. Despite the pain typically associated with grief, navigating its stages can lead to personal growth. Similar to Erikson's stages, the stages of grief provide a framework for comprehending and navigating the grieving process, enabling individuals to integrate the loss into their lives and eventually find a renewed sense of purpose and meaning.

CHAPTER 2

G rief and loss are complex experiences that have been studied from various theoretical perspectives. Several prominent theories and models shed light on the process of grieving and provide frameworks for understanding the different aspects of this journey.

Kübler-Ross's Model proposes five stages of grief, including "denial," "anger," "bargaining," "depression," and "acceptance," illustrating the emotional and psychological progression individuals may undergo. The Dual Process Model emphasizes the oscillation between loss-oriented coping (focusing on the pain of the loss) and restoration-oriented coping (attending to practical life changes).

Worden's Model outlines four tasks of mourning, which involve *"accepting the reality of the loss," "experiencing the pain of grief," "adjusting to life without the deceased,"* and *"finding an enduring connection while moving forward."*

Attachment Theory recognizes the *"ongoing bond with the deceased"* and the *"need to readjust that bond."*

The Continuing Bonds Theory suggests that individuals can maintain a healthy relationship with the dead while adapting to life without them.

Additionally, the *Meaning-Making Model* focuses on finding personal meaning and making sense of the loss experience.

Rando's Six "R" Processes of Mourning provide a comprehensive framework that includes "*recognizing the loss,*" "*reacting to the separation,*" "*recollecting the deceased and the relationship,*" "*relinquishing attachment,*" "*readjusting to a new environment,*" and "*reinvesting in new relationships and pursuits.*"

While these theories offer valuable insights into the grieving process, it's essential to acknowledge that grief is a profoundly personal and individual experience, and individuals may navigate their unique paths through grief and loss.

In the exploration of grief and loss theories, it becomes evident that each theory holds valuable keys to help individuals process and navigate through their experiences of loss, facilitating understanding and personal growth. As I delved into studying these theories, I discovered common threads that also relate to the counseling work I engage in within my practice. It is with this understanding that I have chosen the title "Guerrilla Grief" for this book, aiming to emphasize the notion that there is no one-size-fits-all approach to overcoming grief. Drawing inspiration from the concept of guerrilla warfare, where local farmers became non-traditional warriors to drive out invading armies, we can envision the American Revolution depicted in films like "The Patriot," where outnumbered rebels used unconventional tactics to defeat a formidable British force.

Similarly, individuals facing grief must adapt and utilize any available means to navigate their unique journey. Just like guerrilla warfare, grief can be messy, requiring us to employ all the tools and resources at our disposal. Overcoming grief is not the ultimate goal; rather, it is about integrating grief into our new narrative.

In this grief manual, I aim to highlight practical steps and the main domains that need attention for "men" to move through grief with direction and purpose. These domains encompass the physical, psychological, spiritual, social, resilience, honor, remembrance, and purpose aspects. By embracing and continuously improving these domains, we have a remarkable opportunity to grow and thrive as men, even in the face of devastating losses. This manual will provide practical steps and share real-life anecdotes that exemplify these steps in action.

CHAPTER 3

Purpose is the thing that truly pulls us forward in life. When we have a purpose, we are able to find a way to do the things that feel impossible. As you are moving through your grief journey, you will likely find glimmers of opportunity and purpose that have never occurred to you before. These glimmers may not always feel like purpose, but they are a start. The thing with grief and grieving is that it is one of our most genuine and raw experiences as humans. Grief brings with it sadness, memories, love, pain, connection, and even hope. I attended a funeral a while back of a former supervisor of mine at an old job. We were never really close outside of work but saw one another almost daily and enjoyed regular banter and talking about work-related issues. He was around 60 years old and received a cancer diagnosis. They were hopeful at first and he fought for over a year but eventually, cancer took his life. The pastor at this funeral was a Korean man who had moved to Maine to pastor a church a couple of years before. He spoke about how grief in South Korea was expressed differently than in much of the West. They were more public and emotive with crying and physical expressions of sadness. He said something that really stood out to me, and I repeat it to many of my clients who are in grief. When someone that we love dies, they give us one of the most important gifts that we will ever receive from them; they give us the gift to reflect on our own lives and to genuinely observe if there are things that we would like to be different as we move forward. We can note regrets and successes and evaluate our perception of how life has gone so far. Death is one example, but I find this principle to be true with almost any kind of loss. The loss of a career, a divorce or break up, loss of a home — these are all areas that allow us to reflect on what changes we would like to make in our lives. Too often in life, we as men, struggle with being open and honest with ourselves in times of loss. We may be harsh with ourselves and blame the loss entirely on us, or we may do the opposite and refuse to learn and evaluate where and why things could have been done differently. The loss gives us the opportunity to learn so much when we become open and honest with ourselves. This can evoke some pain, but this genuine state of self-reflection can also create a beautiful opportunity to grow and learn in a whole new unexplored way.

Purpose can feel tricky sometimes, and we can also fall into self-defeating patterns in which we compare our purpose to others. When Joel died, I was still trying to find my purpose in life. At the time I was driven by the prospect of an exciting career in the Executive Protection field. I had made a substantial investment in training and attended and completed a 700+ hour training curriculum to become a protection specialist. I found challenges in breaking into the lucrative side of the field and realized it would take persistence and sacrifice to make this career come to fruition. I made the move to Seattle, largely in part, because the amount of work in the executive protection field was known to be on the West Coast. I moved there knowing only one friend and with little in the amount of savings. I began applying for protection companies and law enforcement positions almost immediately after arriving there. I found work each day to make ends meet while I waited for something to happen with the applications. This was 2007, and it was the first time in my life I had ever heard of Craigslist.

No, it's not what you think, I promise! The first month after my arrival, I logged on to Craiglist nearly every morning and looked in the "HELP WANTED" general labor section. I didn't and still don't possess a specialized skill in the trades, but the one thing I have always been able to rely on has been my stellar work ethic. I found work daily; wheel-barrowing concrete, landscaping, carpentry helper - odds and ends work.

Looking back now, I have no idea what I was thinking. I had left a steady place of employment in Florida to make this move. The company had provided regular security work, but I had felt stifled and knew that they were holding me back from getting into the part of the protection field that truly inspired and motivated me. I knew my purpose was to enter the executive protection field and I was willing to do whatever it took to get there. I recall finding work daily at that time, in my late 20's, and thinking, "I'm okay with this." It wasn't an ideal situation, but I remained motivated. I knew that this situation was temporary and that my higher calling would be realized as long as I kept taking steps forward to fulfill my purpose. I found steady work with a moving company. I was well-suited for this job because I was young and strong.

The Executive Protection (EP) and law enforcement applications began to pay off, and I was receiving calls and interviews and the beginning of background check processes started taking place for several companies. If you've ever worked in one of these fields or a similar field then you are aware of just how long and arduous these processes can often be. I continued with the moving company, the money wasn't bad, and I was content. I knew that my big break was just around the corner. It felt like a bit of a spartan existence, but I embraced it.

I was motivated, energized, and living out the steps of my purpose as a man. Suddenly, it was gone. My world had been shattered. Joel dying, sent me for a loop and confused what I thought my purpose on this earth was supposed to be. I returned to Maine for his funeral in June not knowing or even possessing the ability to process what my next steps would be. I stayed in Maine until August. The calls were coming in to continue with my process for the protection companies, but I could not make sense of how to proceed. I recall being standoffish and uncertain of what to tell them.

Ultimately, I made the decision to move back to Maine. The thought of going back to the grind and hustle of trying to make it on the West Coast had lost its luster. What had been exciting and energizing just a month before, now filled me with dread and uncertainty. I longed to be home and close to family, friends, the outdoors, hunting, the lake, and everything familiar. I didn't realize the journey that I was about to embark on, but I knew it would be different.

After a few months of living back in my childhood home, I made the decision to return to working as a *Correction Officer* in southern Maine. I had left that job nearly four years prior, and I left with prejudice. After just one year of working there, I had become restless and uninspired by the work I was doing. That was what began my journey into the security field. Now four years later, the idea of returning was strangely comforting. A job that I had begun to hate before now offered a sense of security and familiarity. I was good at the job and had made many good friends in my short time there. After yet another lengthy hiring process, I returned and went back to work on overnight shifts.

I still grieved. My return was less than 8 months after Joel had died, and I was still in new grief. I knew that Corrections wasn't my lifelong career choice, but I didn't know what was. As I reflect back, I am able to see clearly that I struggled with the lack of purpose at that time. I didn't know that then. It just felt like I was going through the motions. I occasionally became discouraged and felt as though it was a setback in my life. I knew that I would forge forward as I always had, but I didn't know what that would look like.

A lesson, that I took from my detour to Seattle is that I was resilient and would do whatever it took to advance my purpose when I was aware of what it was. In the meantime, I wholeheartedly subscribed to the ideology that if one keeps pushing in the right direction, then eventually the stars will align and good things will occur. I began dating and after a few months met the woman who would two years later be the mother of my beautiful son, Joel, the namesake of my brother.

As we dated, I returned to school to work on my bachelor's degree in criminology. I had left Maine with around 90 credits, so I needed a couple of years to round out the 120 credits for my bachelor's. I didn't know what I wanted to do with the criminology degree anymore, but it gave me a sense of purpose and pride in the work that I was doing. I would call this stage an *interim purpose.*

Looking back, here is what I make of it. We sometimes get hung up on thinking that our purpose has to be a large, observable, inspiring endeavor or else, it is just not worthwhile. I now know and believe that this cannot be further from the truth. As men, our purpose begins by becoming the best version of ourselves. This is a very practical concept, as it is available for us to embrace every day. We don't have to change the entire world. We just have to be committed to making the world that we live in a little bit better every day.

As we continue to embark on our genuine journey of growth through grief, we are presented daily with opportunities to expand into places that we had not thought were possible in the past. This truly is an exciting time when we grasp the energy that is available to us. *Purpose* is unlimited and infinite and there is a larger purpose that is always just around the corner, wrapped up like a gift waiting for just the right moment when we are ready to receive it. As we work, we are preparing ourselves and becoming the men that we need to be to meet this purpose when it presents itself.

After Joel died, my parents. my dad specifically, found purpose through creating and growing **House in the Woods**. It grew slowly. We brought veterans in small numbers to Maine to experience the healing qualities of the Maine outdoors. My dad hit many obstacles during this time. At one time, the governor of Maine had tasked members of his executive committee, the Commanders' Meeting, and the legislature, to help him with growing and expanding **House in the Woods**. He met with a large group of them, and they continued to tell him the additional tasks that he would have to do before they would be able to help him. He became frustrated by the addition of barriers and red tape until he finally had enough. He finally stood up and scolded them, "Look, the Governor told you to help me get this program going. If you're not going to help, then just get out of the way. I'll do it myself."

That is just what he did.

When a man has a purpose that is so defined and driven, he does not have to do a lot in the means of seeking others to help him in achieving his goals. Purpose-driven focus provides the energy that will effectively bring people to the man to help achieve the purpose. I am not saying that we will never have to reach out or seek counsel or assistance in our journey of fulfilling our purpose. I am saying that working for a purpose that is seeped in genuine passion and done with integrity has a contagious effect and will often impact and draw people in on levels you may have previously felt were impossible.

House in the Woods Military & Family Retreat is an entirely purpose-built endeavor that was created out of the intense and powerful grief we went through after my brother was killed. My dad needed something to feel connected to him. He needed a purpose, and he needed to grieve. As the program grew, so too did our interactions with the wonderful veterans and their family members who have also given so much while serving our country.

I recall receiving a random message one night on our organizational Facebook page from a woman who had attended or was scheduled to attend one of our retreats. She was on the West Coast in Seattle, not far from where I had lived. She was struggling and, at one point, stated that she was suicidal. We chatted for hours, and I helped her find resources that she could reach out to in her area. Before we stopped chatting, she had agreed to contact the crisis line and get the help that she needed to move forward. I was oblivious at the time, but interactions like this and stories from my parents about veterans reaching out to tell them a visit to *House in the Woods* had saved their lives life from suicide were forming the basis of my purpose.

House in the Woods really was and is my father's purpose. It is not my purpose, but it does encompass part of what my purpose is. As I have watched my father overcome obstacles to grow this program, I have seen what it means to have a purpose so steadfast that no obstacle or person can stop you. Our losses can and often do create a powerful catalyst for us to identify and live out our purpose. As *House in the Woods* continued to grow, I continued to give and interact as much as I could. I also remained employed at the jail, finished my bachelor's, and had a son. My beautiful son became the next step in my journey towards my higher calling.

For me, this road was not without its blocks and challenges. With her permission, I am going to speak briefly about my relationship with Joel's mom and how it also helped me to realize my purpose in the most round about unlikely, and frankly, at times, painful way. She and I connected early after we had experienced losses in our lives life that we were still processing, and I might add we each still had a lot of work to do as individuals.

We married and had Joel which was a very happy time for both of us. My grief resurfaced and was displayed often with anger, withdrawal, and even apathy. As any couple, we had adjustment challenges. With hindsight, I can say that my unintegrated grieving process brought a substantial burden into the relationship, particularly when working to manage conflict. Along with individual counseling at times throughout our marriage, we also attempted couples counseling three different times over the course of our marriage. Eventually, the gig was up. We had each created a lot of damage and went from wanting our son to have parents that stayed married, come hell or high water, to having parents that were not at odds and in conflict perpetually. We made the decision to separate and ultimately divorce.

This was a very painful process especially early on. Towards the end of our marriage, before we had decided to end it, I realized how unfulfilled I had been at my Corrections career as well as the landscaping business that I had begun to operate. I did not know what I wanted to do, but I knew that I lacked a sense of purpose in many parts of my life. My son was my purpose, and I needed to model to him what a man living out his purpose really looked like. looks. How a man fulfilled by purpose can change his world.

I became ponderous most days. I reflected back on the times I had been in a counselor's office over the past few years. I had always felt comfortable and nearly always left a session feeling as though I had gained new insight into my life or my relationship. I had learned how to process the grief from my brother's death and, most importantly, I had learned when I needed more support than friends or family could offer.

As I pondered and searched, the counseling offices continued to surface in my mind. So too did the impromptu conversations from the struggling veterans that had attended *House in the Woods*. When I found it, I knew I had no doubt.

Husson University offered a Master's in Clinical Mental Health with a path to licensure as a Licensed Clinical Professional Counselor. I applied and was accepted to this program. At this point, in 2016, I had a very cursory vision of what that journey would look like but from the beginning, it invigorated me.

During the course of this program, I was divorced and moved from the home that we shared. I also dissolved the landscaping company that I had worked hard for several years to build. I was fortunate to have a flexible job as a security officer at a local hospital, and this gave me the opportunity to work around my school schedule. This was also a substantial financial hardship, having gone from a two-income household with a profitable business, to a per diem worker and full-time graduate student.

I worked to integrate my new life. This also included how and when I would spend time with my son. This was very challenging early on, and many nights I spent awake missing him, my former life, and wishing that I could do more to protect him from the negative experience of living in two homes. As challenging as this season of my life was, it still felt right. It can be hard to explain when purpose calls, especially when it's hard to pay the bills, and your identity as a man, parent, and person is challenged and put to the test.

Full disclaimer here: I struggled and there were short periods where it was hard to picture the future. It was as if I had done this before, and by God, my body, and soul knew it. My subconscious drew on my time moving to Seattle and the challenges and the daily grind that ensued. It reminded me that when I had a purpose and a direction, I would do whatever it took to get there. The real difference here, as far as how I internalized this experience, from the past was this time I was responsible for my son. I'm his father and I loved that, and at the same time, it terrified me.

As the purpose goes, *fatherhood* really fueled me. I thought of the life that I wanted for us in years to come. I also thought of my brother, his sacrifice, and how I wanted to honor his memory and legacy. Military service had evaded me and so had the other careers that I had gravitated to. I began to, really deeply, ponder the idea that possibly things were coming to be just as they were meant to be. I had spent years wishing things had gone differently early in my adulthood, yet here I was in the midst of a challenging, trying, and even painful time, and I began to believe that this was no accident. I was here for a reason. I dedicated myself to continuing and completing my education. I sincerely believe that I would never have completed or even begun my journey toward becoming a counselor if I had not had the life that I had had up to that point.

As I write, I have been a therapist for nearly three years. I have found continued reassurance that I made the correct decision to embrace this path in my life. Many doors have opened, and I am confident that they will continue to. Do I feel that I have fulfilled my ultimate calling in this life? Heck no. I do know with complete certainty that I am on a path that is genuine, energizing, and fulfilling to the utmost.

Helping others is one of our ultimate, existential purposes for being on this earth. This certainly does not have to be done in a counseling office., There are so many opportunities to help others when we are looking. When purpose and direction evade us, even temporarily, I find the best thing that I can do is to look genuinely at what I can do to improve my world on this day, in this moment. When we embrace loss as a journey to a greater purpose, we open ourselves to the immense possibility that was not previously accessible. As a younger colleague of mine in the counseling field likes to say to me when she feels I take her sarcasm wrongly, "Don't get it twisted."

So don't get it twisted, I'm not attempting to paint the journey from loss to a higher calling with rose-colored glasses. It is anything but that.

There is pain and processes and growth, along with setbacks, relapse, confusion, and uncertainty. I am, however, here to reassure you that when you learn to grieve your losses with intention and genuineness, you will find the energy and strength to endure and grow where you never felt possible.

Grief has a remarkable way of helping us question the very purpose of our existence. It's a journey that can lead us to reflect on our values, the meaning we derive from our experiences, and the glimmers of opportunity and purpose that emerge amidst the darkness of loss.

Grief is one of our most genuine and raw human experiences. It encompasses a spectrum of emotions, from profound sadness and cherished memories to love, pain, and even hope. While my own journey through grief included the challenging experience of divorce, the lessons learned from it apply universally to anyone grappling with loss.

The process of grieving, whether it's due to the death of a loved one, the end of a relationship, or any significant loss, invites us to engage in deep introspection. It offers us a unique opportunity to reflect on our lives and consider whether there are aspects we wish to change or improve as we move forward. In many ways, the departure of someone we love acts as a catalyst for self-evaluation, where we assess regrets, successes, and our overall life trajectory.

One story that comes to mind here is of a teenage young man that I had worked with. He had a girlfriend that had left him some time before I met him and it was quite devastating at first. This kid was remarkable in that he had some early life experience that could have made it easy for him to feel scorned and generally mad at life. He really presented as the opposite, he was grounded, straightforward, and demonstrated a very giving heart. He described how difficult the breakup was initially and then went on to explain how very quickly and effectively he healed and moved on. "So what is your secret here, buddy? ", I asked him.

"Well," he said, *"I had saved all of my money from my Summer job and bought an old pickup truck that I wanted to fix up and drive when I get my license"*.

He went on to detail how he began to pour all of his attention into fixing that old truck. It became his purpose for that time and really was the catalyst for his healing. The truck energized him, highlighted his talents as a mechanic, and allowed him to shift the focus from his loss to his future. I see his story here as a very practical and tangible effort to navigate a painful loss.

Loss gives us the opportunity to be open and honest with ourselves, even when it's uncomfortable. We might be inclined to blame ourselves entirely for the loss, or conversely, refuse to acknowledge our role in it. However, true growth emerges when we confront our vulnerabilities and evaluate where and how things could have been different. This kind of self-reflection, though often painful, can lead to profound personal growth and learning.

Purpose can be elusive, especially when we compare our journey to others. In my own experience, I was still searching for my purpose when I faced Joel's death. At the time, I was driven by the prospect of an exciting career in Executive Protection, a path that required persistence and sacrifice. I relocated to Seattle in pursuit of this dream, surviving on daily manual labor jobs while awaiting responses to job applications. It was an arduous journey, but it felt right because I knew my purpose was to enter the Executive Protection field.

Despite the less-than-ideal circumstances, I was motivated by the belief that this situation was temporary, and my higher calling was within reach. I found steady work with a moving company, and my persistence paid off as I began receiving calls and interviews from potential employers in the protection field. My journey served as a testament to the power of purpose and persistence.

However, my world was shattered when Joel passed away, leaving me confused about the path I had thought was my purpose. I returned to

Maine, uncertain about my next steps. Eventually, I decided to return to work as a Corrections Officer, a career I had left years earlier. This decision was driven by a lack of clarity about my purpose.

During this period, my purpose became my son. While I didn't know my long-term career path, I realized that being the best version of myself for my child was the immediate purpose I needed. This highlighted the concept that purpose doesn't always have to be a grand, observable endeavor; it can start with being committed to making the world around us a bit better each day.

My parents, particularly my father, discovered their purpose through the creation and growth of **House in the Woods**, a retreat for veterans. This project was born out of intense grief after my brother's death, and my father's unwavering determination to make it a reality was awe-inspiring. His purpose-driven focus was so contagious that it attracted others who wanted to help fulfill that purpose.

When a person is dedicated to a purpose with genuine passion and integrity, it often draws others in, making it easier to achieve the goals. **House in the Woods** exemplifies this concept, showcasing how a steadfast purpose can overcome obstacles and inspire others.

Our losses can serve as powerful catalysts for identifying and living out our purpose. As **House in the Woods** continued to grow, I became increasingly involved, which led me to explore new facets of my purpose. My journey also included returning to school to pursue a degree in criminology, which provided a sense of purpose and pride in my work.

Purpose isn't confined to monumental achievements. It often begins with the commitment to become the best version of ourselves each day. This practical concept is available to us daily, empowering us to improve our world incrementally.

When we embrace loss as a journey toward a greater purpose, we open ourselves to previously inaccessible possibilities. This path is far from easy, marked by pain, growth, setbacks, and uncertainty. Still, as we learn to grieve with intention and authenticity, we discover the strength and energy to endure and grow in ways we never thought possible.

CHAPTER 4 – PHYSICAL

When we experience grief, it affects not only our emotions but also our bodies. It's like a knot that tangles up our insides and makes us feel exhausted and unwell. That's why it's crucial to pay attention to our physical well-being, especially for us men. Sometimes, when we're feeling down, we may be tempted to turn to alcohol or drugs to cope, thinking they'll help us feel better. But in reality, they can make things worse and throw off the balance of chemicals in our bodies. So, let's explore how we can take care of ourselves physically, even amidst challenging times. I am not asserting that you have to be a teetotaller to navigate grief successfully, but I encourage you to be aware and mindful of how substance use may set you back at times in your grief journey.

One essential aspect is nourishing our bodies with good food. When we're grieving, it's common to lose our appetite or reach for unhealthy snacks. However, feeding our bodies nutritious foods provides the fuel they need to stay strong and cope better overall. So, try to choose balanced meals that include fruits, vegetables, lean proteins, and whole grains.

Another vital step is engaging in physical activity. Moving our bodies not only helps us stay fit but also releases tension and boosts our mood. It's like a language through which we communicate with ourselves, letting go of some of the pain we carry inside. Men, in particular, often find solace in physical expression when working through grief. Whether it's chopping wood, running, or engaging in intense workouts, these activities can help us process our emotions and find a sense of release.

I remember a powerful story about my father after my brother Joel died in Iraq. The weight of grief hung heavy on our family, and my father, a strong and stoic man, needed an outlet for his pain. He spent days outside, tirelessly chopping away at the old maple stump in our front yard backyard. With every swing of the axe, it was as if he was releasing the anguish from his heart. The repetitive, physical exertion provided him with a tangible way to channel his emotions and find a temporary respite from the overwhelming sorrow.

For some men, physical activity becomes a form of therapy, allowing them to express their grief and find a sense of control amidst the chaos. Engaging in activities that require physical exertion can be a powerful tool for processing emotions, releasing tension, and finding moments of clarity and peace, whether it's working out, participating in sports, or engaging in outdoor activities. Allow me to introduce you to an extraordinary individual I've had the privilege of meeting on several occasions:

Zack, a Marine who faced the harsh reality of war when an IED explosion in Iraq left him missing significant portions of his legs, hands, and fingers. Zack is not just a survivor, but also a devoted family man, blessed with a loving wife and two beautiful children.

My first encounter with Zack was during one of our *House in the Woods (HITW)* bear hunts, an event designed to provide therapeutic outdoor experiences. What struck me immediately about Zack was his indomitable spirit and an unmistakable zest for life that radiated from him. During that hunt, Zack managed to harvest a large, black bear with the assistance of one of our versatile Action Track Chairs, essentially mini tanks designed to empower individuals with physical challenges to explore the wilderness.

Zack returned for a second year, and this time, he achieved an even greater feat – he harvested a magnificent bull moose with the skilled guidance of my father, who expertly called the bull into their vicinity.

Later, we invited Zack to speak at our annual golf tournament, our largest fundraiser. We believed it was crucial for our attendees to understand the people and causes they were supporting. What struck me the most about Zack's impact was not what I expected. His wife also joined the event and spoke eloquently about Zack's journey after the explosion had taken so much from him. She described a time when Zack was lost in the depths of depression, feeling hopeless and utterly useless. Leaving him was never an option for her, but living with the shadow of his despair was becoming increasingly challenging.

Then, an opportunity arose for a veterans' hunting trip, and she strongly urged Zack to participate. Though reluctant at first, Zack eventually agreed, believing his physical limitations would hinder his enjoyment of the trip. However, on that trip, something transformative happened. Zack not only harvested an animal, but he also actively participated in the skinning, meat processing, and camp chores. When he returned, his wife noticed a newfound confidence in him, a spark that she hadn't seen since before the explosion. That hunting trip became the catalyst for Zack's journey toward rediscovering his sense of purpose.

As I mentioned earlier, Zack is nothing short of remarkable. He went on to become a member of the American Sled Hockey team and even participated in the Boston Marathon wheelchair race. In 2022, Zack achieved an incredible feat by winning the Boston Marathon. Yet, what sets him apart is his humility and unwavering commitment to his family. He embarked on his path to healing and ultimately shone as brightly as a star, all because he made that initial choice to get out there and simply move.

What resonates with you and gives you a healthy outlet to work through your grief?

In challenging times, substance use and chemical dysregulation can become hurdles to our well-being. Alcohol and drugs might offer temporary relief, but they can disrupt our body's natural balance and make it harder to heal. It's important to recognize these risks and seek healthier alternatives for managing our emotions and finding support.

Taking care of our bodies also involves seeking professional help. Professionals, like counselors or doctors specializing in grief, can guide us through the physical challenges we may encounter. They can provide strategies, exercises, and techniques tailored to our unique needs, helping us regain balance and navigate the complexities of grief more effectively.

Furthermore, quality sleep is a crucial ally in our healing journey. Grief often disrupts our sleep patterns, making it harder to rest peacefully. Establishing a consistent bedtime routine and creating a relaxing sleep environment can promote better sleep. Consider practices such as deep breathing, meditation, or listening to calming music before bed to help your mind unwind and promote a more restorative sleep.

Remember, self-care is not just about our emotional well-being; it also encompasses caring for our bodies. By nourishing ourselves with healthy food, engaging in physical activity, seeking professional support, and prioritizing quality sleep, we can build strength and resilience during tough times. This chapter is here to guide you in understanding the importance of physical well-being and equip you with strategies to take care of your body while navigating grief. By honoring your physical needs and making self-care a priority, you can cultivate inner strength and find a healthier path forward in your grief journey, just as my father found solace in chopping that old maple stump.

In the previous section, we explored the significance of physical exercise in grief healing. Now, let us delve into the profound impact of Brazilian Jiu-Jitsu (BJJ), in my personal journey through grief. For over 15 years, BJJ has not only provided me with a form of exercise but also a strategic outlet akin to chess and a supportive social community. In this section, I will share how my involvement in BJJ and weightlifting has become an integral part of my grief healing process, offering both physical and emotional benefits.

The Physical and Mental Aspects of Brazilian Jiu-Jitsu:

Brazilian Jiu-Jitsu is a martial art that combines self-defense techniques and grappling on the ground. Engaging in BJJ offers a holistic form of exercise that benefits both the body and mind. The physical demands of BJJ enhance cardiovascular fitness, strength, and flexibility, contributing to overall physical well-being. The mental aspect of BJJ involves strategic thinking, problem-solving, and anticipation—much like a game of chess. This mental stimulation provides a valuable distraction from grief-related thoughts and allows for a focused mindset.

The Release of Stress and Distraction from Pain:

One of the significant aspects of BJJ, as a grief healing tool, is its ability to provide a physical release from stress and a distraction from pain. When engaging in intense training sessions or grappling matches, the focus shifts entirely to the present moment. The adrenaline rush and physical exertion allow for a temporary escape from the overwhelming emotions associated with grief. BJJ serves as an outlet to channel negative energy, frustrations, and pent-up emotions, providing a cathartic release that can be profoundly therapeutic.

The Social Support and Sense of Community:

Grief can often make us feel isolated and disconnected from others. Engaging in BJJ offers a unique opportunity to build relationships within a supportive community. Training alongside like-minded individuals fosters a sense of camaraderie and support, creating a space where one can share their grief journey with others who understand and empathize. The bond formed through training partners and coaches can provide a network of emotional support, encouragement, and understanding that is invaluable during times of loss.

Weightlifting and its Complementary Benefits:

In addition to my involvement in BJJ, I also engage in regular weight-lifting as part of my grief-healing routine. Weightlifting provides a different form of physical challenge and strength development. The act of lifting weights can be empowering, instilling a sense of accomplishment and resilience. Moreover, the physical fitness benefits derived from weightlifting complement the demands of BJJ, enhancing overall performance and preventing injury. The combination of BJJ and weightlifting creates a well-rounded approach to physical exercise and grief healing.

The inclusion of Brazilian Jiu-Jitsu and weightlifting in my grief-healing journey has been transformative. BJJ offers a unique blend of physical exercise, strategic thinking, and social support, which together contribute to emotional and mental well-being. Engaging in intense training sessions, experiencing the release of stress, and finding distraction from pain have become crucial aspects of my healing process. The supportive community within BJJ and the complementary benefits of weightlifting have played an integral role in nurturing resilience, finding purpose, and progressing toward a place of solace amidst grief. I encourage you to explore physical activities that resonate with you, as I have with BJJ, and allow them to become vital components of your grief-healing journey. Choose what works for you and stick with it consistently. Your physical health is an important component of your ability to heal from grief. I am, by no means, saying here that you are required to rush out and join a BJJ gym. However, I strongly encourage you to adopt a regular exercise routine that is doable for the long term and something that you enjoy.

Nature and our physical health also go hand in hand. I recently observed a presentation by a former classmate who cited the physical benefits of "*playing with dirt*." Being connected to the earth is good for us. Bare feet on the grass, a walk in nature, a visit to the water, all of these actions offer the opportunity to become more grounded, and more grounded equals more regulated. At **House in the Woods (HITW)** our veteran guests visit the woods of Maine for hunting, fishing, and recreational trips. Being in the outdoors is recharging. Part of my research in graduate school was focused on reviewing literature that explored the benefits of outdoor experiences in helping with symptoms of PTSD. One of the primary studies that was conducted, evaluated a fly-fishing experience for veterans through the Veterans Administration. The evaluators measured PTSD symptoms before, during, and after the event. Most of the attendees showed marked improvement, or decrease in their symptoms even months after the event. There are numerous opportunities to connect physical activity, physical healing, and nature so the important part here is to just begin to move and to embrace opportunity.

CHAPTER 5 – REMEMBER AND ACKNOWLEDGE

In this exploration, we delve into the significance of commemorating items of loss. When faced with death, we honor the departed through funeral services, conversations, memories, cards, and floral tributes. Funerals serve as a poignant means to navigate grief and mourning, allowing us to publicly recognize the weight of our loss and the pain of missing our loved ones. These gatherings extend a network of support and offer avenues to share our anguish. By revealing our pain to others, we invite them to bear witness to our journey, a crucial step in processing our loss. The compassion and attendance of others contribute to the validation of our sorrow, reminding us that our grief is both meaningful and acknowledged.

In my perspective, the U.S. military demonstrates an exceptional commitment to honoring and remembering those who have fallen. A full honors funeral for a fallen soldier is a profound spectacle. The discipline displayed by the soldiers involved in the ceremony, the meticulous folding of the flag, the solemnity of the 21-gun salute – collectively, these elements convey a resounding message of honor and respect for the individual's service to the nation. As a family member grappling with the loss of a soldier, witnessing such reverence provides solace, reassurance, and a sense of pride in knowing that your loved one's sacrifice is recognized and cherished.

Equally important is the practice of remembering and honoring other forms of loss. In cases of relationship dissolution, particularly breakups, or divorces, it is not uncommon, especially among men, to adopt a façade of stoicism, attempting to downplay the impact of the loss. Phrases like "it was a waste of time" or "they meant nothing to me" may arise as defenses. While it's true that some relationships may harbor negative memories, such as instances of abuse, it's important to recognize these as exceptions.

Even in scenarios where we did not desire the end of the relationship, it's essential to acknowledge the value that person brought into our lives. They shared their time, love, and affection, offering us a part of their invaluable presence. This acknowledgment doesn't imply distorting the past through rose-tinted glasses; rather, it underscores the necessity of gleaning lessons from that connection. To heal and progress, we must release the hold of resentment, opting instead, for a decision to relinquish spite and hatred. These emotions hinder growth. Forgiveness, where appropriate, and releasing what we can, while extracting the lessons offered, paves the way for healing and transformation.

In the tapestry of life, each thread of remembrance is woven with care. Funerals and military honors, recollections, and reflections – these are the threads that guide us through the labyrinth of grief. Just as a quilt is stitched together, our process of remembrance forms a coherent narrative that supports our healing journey. It's a tribute to the human spirit's resilience and its capacity to grow from even the most profound losses. Through the act of remembering and honoring, we honor, not only the past but also the boundless potential of our own growth.

As we remember, we also gain the opportunity to let go of some of the bad things about our lost object. Resentment and hate are killers, and they, are all too often, lurking in the shadow of any unintegrated loss. Holding on to resentment does not allow us to move forward in an efficient way. By harboring resentment, we risk becoming obsessed with our loss. Even in death, we often have regrets or unfinished business with the deceased. We must do something with those feelings, or they will continue to keep us stuck.

In my personal experience with the loss of my brother, I found phases of regret and resentment toward the U.S. government for sending him to die. At the same time, I had feelings of immense pride for his service as a selfless act. To quote the verse on his headstone, "Greater love has no man than this, that he lay down his life for his friend." Wow! What a way to be remembered! Sorting out regret and resentment has been a large part of my process. Allowing myself to release from things I have no control over was a changing point in my healing journey. It allowed me to honor my brother wholeheartedly while still having concerns and frustrations about the war that took him from me. The same concept applies to all types of losses. While the specifics are different, the principles remain steadfast. Honor and remember the value that was brought to your life from that person, career, relationship, or object, and allow yourself to learn and grow from the aspects that are painful.

Memories of our lost loved ones aren't always, nor should they always be, exclusively positive. Accurate and realistic recollections, along with reflection, enable us to process loss in a manner that aligns with reality, fostering congruence between our emotional and logical thoughts. Often, our memories are tainted by extremes, either portraying the person or thing with excessive fondness or extreme discontent. A good rule of thumb is that extreme thinking is often, though not always, inaccurate at best. Different types of grief and loss experiences may require varying approaches for adjusting our memories over time. For instance, in the event of a loved one's death, recalling fondness is one of the more helpful memory patterns we can experience.

As I reminisce about my life with my brother before his passing, I am logically aware that we had moments of hardship and brief disagreements. However, these memories do not take precedence in how I have integrated his death into my life moving forward. Fondly remembering our relationship and his presence has encouraged me to embrace his short time on Earth as a beautiful part of our human experience. There were times, especially early on, when his death felt all-encompassing when I felt overly attached to my own identity. When we allow one person or thing to entirely define our identity, it can be extremely challenging to move forward in life. We might feel a lack of importance, question our self-worth, or fear forgetting and dishonoring the memory of our loved ones.

During these times, my task was to find the balance between my logical and emotional memories. To achieve this, I recalled his time alive on Earth. Despite his significant presence in my life, he did not define me as an individual. Especially in adulthood, when he joined the Army, and I began building my own life, we had our separate identities. Although our lives intersected, sometimes more than others, we remained individuals. When someone or something leaves our life and we feel unable to move on without them, we must question the validity of that feeling. With my brother, I discovered that integrating his loss meant finding congruence between my emotional and logical memories of him as a path to move forward. This concept applies, and perhaps even more so, to job or career loss, break-ups, divorce, or other types of loss that make us feel abandoned or isolated, as if we are nothing without that person or thing.

Another aspect of remembering a lost loved one is *intentionality* and *selectiveness*. Initially, following a loss, we often become consumed by memories of that person or thing. As time passes, these periods of not thinking or remembering become more frequent, which is natural and valuable in our journey forward. Early loss can feel like a time of crisis and dysregulation. As we become more regulated, our logical and emotional memories develop the ability to balance one another. Our goal is not, nor should it be, to trick ourselves into forgetting what we have lost and are grieving, but rather to move in and out of our memories and thoughts in a way that allows us to begin the healing process.

Over the last 15 years since my brother's passing, I have experienced many phases of this process. Occasions like death anniversaries, birthdays, and holidays often bring memories to the forefront and are intentionally explored during family gatherings or individual moments of reflection.

After my brother Joel's death in Iraq due to an IED, I was fortunate to have memories shared by some of his comrades. I believe that sharing these memories and experiences with him was as important for them as it was for me. I vividly recall a conversation about eight months after Joel's death with one of his Sergeants who had been there when he died. It's worth noting that several people from Joel's military service have become like a family to me due to the closeness forged through sharing such a loss. On this night, Sgt. Lyle Walker became the first of many new additions to my family as the closeness we share feels more similar to brotherhood than any other relationship that I could use to explain it.

During our conversation, he shared how long he had known Joel, what Joel meant to him as a friend and a person, and the significance of their relationship. He then described the details and memories of Joel's death, how he was behind Joel's Humvee in a tank on that fateful day when the bomb exploded beneath Joel's vehicle as he manned the .50 caliber machine gun on top. The explosion was devastating, and Joel, along with three of his comrades and an Iraqi interpreter, was in the vehicle when the bomb detonated. The Sergeant explained that Joel was thrown from the vehicle and was still alive but unconscious. It was evident that he would not survive, and the Sergeant described seeing his eyes flutter as he left this earth.

"All I could do was hold his hand as he died," he said.

I sat with a complete stranger who shared the details of Joel's death with emotional yet strangely logical clarity. There was beauty in the sharing of this memory. I recall feeling thankful that in his final moments, Joel had someone who loved him to hold his hand. At that moment, I was overcome with gratitude more than sorrow. It was an unusual experience but profoundly impactful nonetheless.

Nearly 15 years later, I had a similar experience with another of Joel's Sergeant Oscar Ayala who served alongside him and was present when he died. He and his family traveled to Maine to spend time with us on the 15th anniversary of Joel's death and our mother's birthday. On the first night of his visit, as we all gathered in the common area of the *House in the Woods*, he once again described Joel's death. He stood close to me as he spoke, and the room was filled with emotion. I reached for his hand as he spoke, and tears welled up in everyone's eyes as we listened to him recount my brother's final moments. Oscar is a man's man, built tough from life, war, fighting, and wrestling. He went to Ranger school at 40 years old just to check it off his bucket list. But as he spoke now about my brother he was all heart. It was a truly beautiful experience. Oscar and I bonded that week, spending time at the lake and sharing stories of past and future goals. I had gained another brother.

About a year ago, on one of **House in the Woods** bear hunts, I was fortunate to share a bunk room for a night with one of Joel's good buddies from the army, Brandon Benton. I met Brandon in Texas years ago along with Oscar at a Ft. Hood memorial for fallen soldiers. We have stayed in contact over the years but have not been in person. On this night, we talked into the wee hours. We are Facebook friends. I keep up with him and his family on social media, but we haven't really connected like this. He shared what his life had been like since the military, some of the ups and downs of his beautiful family, his struggles with PTSD, and some of the guilt that he held from returning home when my brother and many others from their unit did not. This conversation was cathartic. He shared the memories of their good times and how they were deployed together, but he wasn't on the mission that day. The news devastated him, and the loss felt unbearable. However, as is with active duty deployment, there is little time to grieve and memorialize, the mission is the focus. On this time, 14 years later, he and I shared memories that helped us heal and connect on another level.

On another occasion, Joel's First Sergeant 1ˢᵗ Sgt. Steven Burke and his son-in-law Peter Cooper, who also served with Joel, visited us in Maine. We spent time at the lake and laughed and shared memories. These men felt like family for years. They were at Joel's funeral and the First Sergeant did his memorial presentation both at the funeral and at Ft. Hood, Texas. On this visit, they shared how much they valued my brother as a man, a fellow soldier, and a solid human. One described their first deployment together and how they shared a bunk room. Joel would go to the room, play his guitar, read his Bible, and fall into a peaceful sleep. He described his sleep as only the kind that someone with a clean conscience is truly able to find. Another experience here, where we laughed, we cried, we honored, and remembered. Together, we healed.

There is another important aspect about memory and our own identity I should emphasize here. While we are not, by any means, without an identity after the loss of a person or thing, it is also important to acknowledge how the object of loss has helped to shape our identity. This acknowledgment allows us to integrate loss in a way that is more meaningful. Again, there is balance here, in that, the loss is not our entire identity, but it does shape part of who we are. A healthy loss trajectory is one that acknowledges all facets of loss and takes what we need to help us heal and grow.

I must emphasize that these experiences, while profoundly significant and appreciated, are not daily, weekly, monthly, or even yearly occurrences anymore. In fact, it would not be healthy for any of us to relive these memories with such intensity on a regular basis. There comes a point where memorializing can become overwhelming and stifling. To allow healing, we must allow memories to flow as they naturally do, and this means releasing them when necessary.

CHAPTER 6 – RESILIENCE

What propels us beyond the seemingly insurmountable chasm of grief? How do we reach the other side of sorrow, where hope and healing reside? In these moments of darkness, when loss threatens to engulf us, it is motion, momentum, and movement that guide us forward. The concept of resilience, once used to test the strength of steel, holds valuable lessons. Steel, when subjected to intense heat, forging, cooling, and pressure, displays its resilience by returning to its original state after the ordeal. In contrast, steel lacking this quality bends, breaks, or fails to recover from the relentless pressure.

As men grappling with grief, we undergo our own trials by fire. Loss exerts relentless pressure, pushing us to the brink of bending, if not breaking. Emotions are powerful but not always reliable guides. They are valid and must be acknowledged, yet they do not define us. I've personally felt the weight of pressure so intense it seemed inevitable that I would shatter. But here's the remarkable news, my fellow grieving men – **I DID NOT BREAK.**

After the loss of my brother Joel, a divorce, the loss of my home, career setbacks due to a childhood eye injury, and a painful breakup, there were moments, days, weeks, and months when the pressure felt unbearable. I struggled to see beyond the pain that was consuming me. Looking back on those times, I recognized a pivotal moment that began to turn the tide, gradually guiding me back toward safety and normalcy. It was a moment of questioning, of contemplating what it truly meant to break.

Death, the ultimate breaking point, has likely crossed the minds of many of us as a possible release from the agony of loss. I, too, contemplated it, but I found my answer unsatisfactory. Let me emphasize this, my friend, as you read these words: **DEATH IS NOT THE ANSWER.** As you embark on the journey of resilience, understand that its foundation lies in doing what is necessary to survive. If you ever believe that suicide is your only option, **PLEASE STOP READING NOW**, pick up the phone, and call the national suicide hotline. Know that every person who has held this book and every word written here is rooting for you. I am rooting for you. You are on the precipice of a new, fulfilling life, and you are currently engaged in a fierce battle to take that next step in your journey. You will live. You will thrive. You will be okay. Right now, you are deploying all your resources in *"a guerrilla"* warfare for your life. You deserve to live, to feel alive. Your loved ones deserve you to live and thrive. If you can't pick up the phone for yourself, do it for somebody else.

In my experience, there were times when my will to keep going came from sources external to myself. Becoming a father, my beautiful son, named after my brother Joel, became my ultimate motivation. It was also other people – my family, my parents, my loving sister, and my friends. Over time, as I continued to nurture resilience, the number of people I found as motivations to live and thrive multiplied. In this ongoing process, I have also become a primary motivator for my own life. I have so much to live for that the thought of self-destruction is not even on the table. But there were times when it was. This is warfare, and by definition, war is not fair. As long as we are not harming ourselves or others, no options should be off the table. Fight like you've never fought before. This is resilience – taking the next step to reach the next step until it no longer feels like such an arduous task. There will be moments when it's harder and moments when it's easier.

What Makes Us Resilient?

Resilience and toughness, though related, are not the same. One need not be physically tough to cultivate resilience. I would argue that we are born with some biopsychosocial resilience factors, but these are not one-size-fits-all solutions. Resilience demands practice, patience, and time to build new neurological pathways that demonstrate the benefits of developing a resilient response to life's challenges.

Two stories come to mind when I need a dose of humor and strength to bolster my journey of resilience during moments of discouragement or despair. After Joel's tragic passing, we held a grand funeral for him in the Lee Academy Gymnasium, a place where he, my sister, my grandparents, aunts, and uncles had all once been. In a town of roughly 800 people, over 1,000 mourners gathered. Distinguished guests included the Governor of Maine, two Senators, Representatives, Generals, and fellow military personnel, all of whom I deeply admired. Among them was my cousin Jeremy, a First Sergeant. Joel's unit had replaced Jeremy in Iraq, where he had faced gunfire, been shot in his throat armor, and endured significant losses during his deployment. When the military informed us that Joel's body would receive a military escort from Maryland to Maine for burial, we specifically requested Jeremy, and he graciously accepted the responsibility.

The day the plane arrived at Bangor Airport, a small group of us, composed of close family members, aunts, uncles, and cousins, waited in anticipation. As the plane's cargo door opened, an indelible moment unfolded before our eyes. Jeremy, along with other soldiers and pilots, disembarked and stood at attention. Though we were near, we couldn't reach out or speak. It was Jeremy's solemn duty to escort his fellow soldier and his baby cousin home. What emerged from the cargo door was an image forever etched in my memory: a casket draped in the American flag, cradling my baby brother and an honorable U.S. soldier who had made the ultimate sacrifice.

Returning to the funeral itself, I had wanted to speak in front of the crowd about my brother, although public speaking was never my forte.

My emotions vacillated between numbness and an overwhelming out-pouring of grief. Upon entering the gymnasium and surveying the multitude of people, Jeremy, with an air of brotherly affection, looked at me and said,

"When you get up there and speak, don't cry like a little bitch."

His words, spoken in the true spirit of love, could only come from a best friend or a brother, and they served to ease my anxiety. Another moment during the funeral is etched in my memory — I glanced at the bleachers and saw my childhood friend sitting there. He made a subtle gesture and a facial expression that triggered unexpected laughter. Inappropriately timed but greatly needed, that touch of dark yet loving humor helped to alleviate some of the emotional weight. Resilience is like this; it can be daunting, and sometimes, humor is the lifeline that propels you to the next step of resilience, even when it feels impossible.

These four simple words, **"Just pick it up,"** have been my guiding light through the darkest moments since Joel's passing. When a service member dies, their family faces the solemn privilege and duty of choosing a final resting place, be it a national or state military cemetery or a location of their own choosing. We decided on our town's cemetery, where generations of our family lay at rest. The military funeral, complete with full honors, presented an opportunity for me to be one of the pallbearers for Joel's casket. I approached my family and the military liaison, seeking permission. They granted it, but doubt began to creep in.

The persistent question echoed in my mind: *"What if you drop him in front of everyone?"* This fear gripped me, a gnawing worry that I might mishandle the casket, tarnishing Joel's funeral and bringing shame upon my family, my brother, and our community. My mother sensed my unease and conveyed it to Hervey Clay, the experienced funeral director and Vietnam veteran who had guided us through the process, including viewing Joel's body. Hervey was a man of both strength and kindness, providing reassurance to all who sought his services. On that day, Hervey looked at me as I expressed my concerns, and he uttered four simple, powerful words:

"JUST PICK IT UP!"

Those words, coming from that man at that moment, triggered a profound shift in my perspective. Those words, that lesson, have carried me through countless, seemingly insurmountable challenges in my life. When things have felt impossible, when I've stood on the precipice of falling apart, when I've questioned whether I had the strength to continue, **"Just pick it up"** has resounded in my mind. These words have become my personal resilience mantra. If you don't already have your own resilience mantra for when life's challenges seem overwhelming, I strongly encourage you to find one. You're also welcome to adopt mine: **"Just pick it up"** and keep moving forward. You've got this.

The story of **House in the Woods (HITW)** is filled with themes of resilience, especially in its early days as I witnessed my father surmount barriers to transform his vision into reality. One significant hurdle was obtaining a 501(c)(3) nonprofit designation. We had engaged an attorney to assist, yet the IRS repeatedly rejected our proposal over seemingly trivial objections. This became a costly and frustrating ordeal. After the third rejection, my father had had enough. Against the advice of legal counsel, he took matters into his own hands. He contacted the IRS himself, specifically reaching out to an office in California, known for making significant decisions. On that call, he insisted on speaking to the most senior supervisor available, and he got just that. The gentleman on the other end, a seasoned IRS employee and a fellow Vietnam veteran, not only granted our request but also expressed heartfelt condolences for Joel's loss. Within a month, we had the necessary paperwork.

Another resilience story from **HITW's** early days involved my father speaking before then-Governor John Baldacci. He shared the story of **HITW**, leaving a profound impression on the governor. Without hesitation, Governor Baldacci wrote a $25,000 check from his contingency fund and pledged to find further support for the cause. He assembled a group of state senators and representatives to facilitate **HITW's** growth within the constraints of state government. However, when it came time for a meeting at the Capitol to discuss their progress, my father found himself facing a seemingly one-sided conversation. They repeatedly asked what he had done on his end and presented numerous barriers to providing assistance. After enduring this for a while, my father had had enough. He stood up and declared, "Look, the Governor asked you to help me, and all I'm hearing are reasons why you can't. So if this is how it's going to be, here's my response, **Just get out of my way; I'll do it myself!**" That marked the end of the meeting. While he did eventually receive some state support and fostered a positive relationship with Maine Veterans Affairs, the journey to create *House in the Woods* was a testament to his unwavering determination and resilience in the face of obstacles. In both instances, the mission was too vital to be deterred by perceived barriers. Tenacity and resilience prevailed, and *House in the Woods* became a reality despite the hardships.

As the funeral neared, the discussions revolved around how to honor Joel's service by symbolically bringing him back to his roots. In high school, when my grandfather passed away on New Year's Day, we faced a similar situation. With the ground in Maine frozen solid, we had no choice but to dig his grave by hand. My father, cousins, uncles, and I had wielded shovels, laboring to create a six-foot-deep resting place. We decided to do the same for Joel, not out of obligation but out of love and a deep-seated need to return him to his family and hometown. This act of shared effort bestowed a sense of pride and purpose, uniting us in our grief while honoring Joel's memory. It was an act of resilience in its own right – an acknowledgment that amidst the haze of sorrow, we could still find purpose.

Early in grief, resilience often manifests in seemingly small tasks. The monumental effort of taking a shower and getting dressed for the day can feel like scaling a mountain. And that's perfectly fine. In the psychological context presented earlier in this book, you'll recognize the dorsal state of the nervous system. This state, akin to a dark cave, characterizes our existence in the early stages of grief, where functioning becomes an overwhelming challenge. You may linger in this cave for a time, but eventually, you will move beyond its shadows, if only for moments that grow longer and more frequent.

Acknowledge that your loss has made daily functioning more demanding. Be gentle with yourself and celebrate your efforts, particularly in those early days. Make a game of it, counting how many small things you can achieve in a day – brushing your teeth, combing your hair, tending to the lawn, doing dishes, preparing a meal. These are all acts of resilience when you find yourself in the dorsal state of the nervous system. Understand that some days will be more challenging than others. On occasion, you might choose to remain under the covers all day, and that's okay. Tell yourself, "*Today, I am staying in bed because this is what I need.*" By acknowledging this choice, you empower yourself, reminding yourself that you are in control of your body, and on this day, you have chosen rest, free from guilt.

The beautiful thing about resilience is that eventually, it doesn't feel like work. As you move from hard to easy, dark to light, drained to energized, dorsal to ventral, resilience feels more like a reward. A gift of grit that we give to ourselves that allows us to develop into the new, growth mindset-inspired version of ourselves. I will be so bold as to say that resilience does not always guarantee a specific result, but by God, it guarantees results that are good for us and make us whole, and when you do it for yourself and those people that you love, resilience never fails.

Grief is a complex and deeply personal experience, and it often leads to a re-evaluation of our social connections. In Maslow's hierarchy of needs, social belonging is a fundamental human requirement. When we are grieving, we can find ourselves uncertain about who to rely on as we navigate this new, post-loss world. Sometimes, the loss is a person, be it through death, the end of a friendship, a career change, or a shift in living circumstances. When our social structure is disrupted, it's another form of loss that deserves acknowledgment.

In the pursuit of understanding grief, I embarked on a path that led me from the world of security and corrections to the realm of mental health counseling. My journey was anything but straightforward, filled with unexpected turns and profound insights. This chapter chronicles my transformation from a security professional to a counselor and underscores the pivotal role that therapy plays in navigating the complex terrain of grief.

My early adulthood was marked by a series of roles in security and corrections. My passion for martial arts drew me to careers emphasizing physical prowess and resilience. I worked as a bouncer and corrections officer for seven years and even became a certified bodyguard in the field of executive protection and security. But amidst these roles, there was an unfulfilled sense of purpose.

In my early twenties, I aspired to join the U.S. Border Patrol, receiving a conditional job offer to work on the Mexican border. However, this dream was shattered due to my one-eye condition. It was a devastating blow, and it left me searching for a career that truly resonated with my soul. None of my previous roles had ever felt like the right fit.

After the loss of my brother, Joel, I decided to return to Maine and find stability by working at the jail where I had previously been employed. While it offered comfort and stability, it wasn't long before I realized that something was amiss. Life became unmanageable, and I spiraled into a deep depression. My resentment towards inmates for being alive while my brother had passed away was consuming me. I knew I needed help, but I didn't know where to turn.

Then, I recalled seeing the Employee Assistance Program sign at work, offering mental health counseling as an option. Counseling had never been on my radar, but I decided to take a chance. I attended several sessions with a licensed social worker, and it was a game-changer. A weight was lifted off my shoulders. She encouraged me to leverage my strengths, explore dating, release relationship baggage, and continue to define my life's purpose. Though I don't recall all the details, I distinctly remember feeling like everything would be okay.

As the years went by, I encountered grief again, but this time, I knew when and how to seek help. My marriage became strained, and though we ultimately divorced, couples counseling provided valuable insights. These experiences ignited my interest in becoming a counselor. At 36, I applied and was accepted into the Husson University graduate program for mental health counseling. The journey had just begun.

CHAPTER 7 -
PSYCHOLOGICAL/EMOTIONAL

While my initial goal was to work with veterans and first responders, my internship exposed me to diverse populations, each grappling with their unique grief experiences. When I was licensed and established my practice, I realized that grief was a common thread weaving through many of my clients' lives. Often, they were unaware of the profound impact grief had on them, extending far beyond death to encompass trauma, job loss, betrayal, housing changes, and the empty nest syndrome.

Graduate school introduced me to a myriad of counseling theories, each with its strengths and weaknesses. During my internship, I was asked to identify the counseling theories that resonated most with my style and approach. I chose cognitive behavioral therapy (CBT) and existential therapy, both of which continue to influence my practice.

CBT: Rewriting Thought Patterns

Cognitive Behavioral Therapy (CBT) became a cornerstone of my therapeutic approach. At its core, CBT provides a framework for recognizing and reframing challenging thought patterns. The theory's foundation lies in the ABCs – an event leads to a thought, which generates a feeling, ultimately resulting in an action.

For instance, consider failing a critical exam. The thought "I'm stupid" can evoke feelings of self-pity and inadequacy, leading to a cycle of self-doubt. An alternative thought like "I didn't study enough for this exam" can evoke feelings of hopefulness and motivation, leading to constructive action.

CBT is a valuable tool for navigating grief because it helps individuals confront shame, guilt, self-doubt, and low confidence often associated with significant losses. It teaches us to challenge self-defeating thoughts, allowing us to develop healthier thought patterns and outcomes.

Albert Ellis and Aaron Beck, pioneers of CBT, remind us not to "should" all over ourselves or engage in "musterbation." These terms caution against dismissing our genuine feelings by convincing ourselves that we **should** or **must** feel differently than we actually do. In grief, simply telling ourselves to move on or be over a loss rarely works. Feelings are always valid and must be acknowledged for true processing.

Existential Therapy: Finding Meaning Amidst Loss

Existential therapy, inspired by Victor Frankl's profound insights in "Man's Search for Meaning," emphasizes the significance of our thoughts about a situation. Frankl, a Holocaust survivor, discovered meaning even in the darkest of times. He found purpose in imagining his wife seeing the same stars as he did while in a concentration camp, providing him the strength to endure.

Existentialism plays a pivotal role in identifying and securing our purpose and meaning, even in the most challenging circumstances. This is particularly relevant in my work with incarcerated individuals. Many of them have committed grave deeds, but they too can find purpose and redemption, much like anyone navigating grief.

Imprisonment, the ultimate loss of freedom, can become an opportunity for growth and purpose. If men can find meaning in prison, those facing various forms of loss can do the same.

Polyvagal Therapy: Regulating the Nervous System

Polyvagal therapy, a theory I often use with grieving clients, posits that there are three states of the nervous system: ventral, sympathetic, and dorsal. Each state corresponds to different physiological and emotional experiences.

- Ventral: This state represents openness, creativity, connection, and problem-solving. It's akin to a warm, inviting park bench on a beautiful spring day.

- Sympathetic: This state is associated with fight or flight responses, triggered in moments of danger or high stress, like encountering a bear on your front porch.

- Dorsal: The dorsal state is our most primitive, a place of paralysis, shock, despair, and trauma. It's the dark cave where we sometimes find ourselves.

While there's no right or wrong way to grieve, a healthy grieving process involves moving through these states over time. Staying in the sympathetic or dorsal state is akin to being stuck in grief or trauma. A polyvagal therapist can teach you to navigate these states effectively, helping you process and feel your loss fully.

The Therapist's Role: Unburdening and Regulation

When individuals seek counseling, they are often in a state of dysregulation. A therapist's primary goal is to provide a temporary presence for clients to regulate themselves, acquire coping skills, process emotions, and return to a state of daily functioning.

In therapy, you can unburden your soul. While therapy is not the sole solution for healing, it is a valuable tool. It allows you to learn and grow, providing a safe space to share your pain and begin processing it. Think of a therapist as a guide, similar to a Maine Guide leading you through the North Maine Woods. While you could embark on the adventure alone, a guide's knowledge enhances the experience, ensuring you don't miss the hidden gems along the way.

Narrative Therapy: Writing Your Grief Story

Narrative therapy, like journaling on steroids, guides clients through writing about their loss experience. It starts with general writing about the loss and gradually delves into emotions and feelings associated with the loss. Writing can trigger a cathartic release of pent-up emotions, allowing them to flow freely.

While it's possible to navigate narrative therapy alone, the guidance of a skilled therapist or trusted mentor can enhance the experience, making it more fluid and less confusing.

Sharing Your Grief: The Power of Connection

We need to be heard; it's a fundamental human need. Sharing our grief through therapy, with friends, family, support groups, blogging, writing, physical expression, prayer, and meditation can be profoundly transformative. Therapists are trained to receive and release raw grief in a session. While friends and family play a significant role in our grief experience, they often lack the training to handle the intensity of emotions shared in therapy.

Breaking the Stigma: Seeking Help

Despite the stigma around men seeking counseling, I encourage you to take the leap if you're considering it. Your journey is yours alone, and seeking help is a sign of strength, not weakness. Therapy can be life-changing, not only for you but also for the people who love and look up to you. Motivation to seek help can come from within or from the desire to strengthen your relationships and inspire others to seek help when needed.

In the next chapter, we'll explore the importance of support networks, self-care, and the significance of men sharing their grief experiences openly. Remember, healing is a journey, and seeking help is a vital step toward reclaiming your emotional well-being.

CHAPTER 8 - SOCIAL

In Maslow's hierarchy of needs, "social belonging" is a fundamental human requirement. When we are grieving, we can find ourselves uncertain about who to rely on as we navigate this new, post-loss world. Sometimes, the loss is a person, be it through death, the end of a friendship, a career change, or a shift in living circumstances. When our social structure is disrupted, it's another form of loss that deserves acknowledgment.

During grief, some of our friends may step back, leaving us feeling isolated. Grief is a powerful and often overwhelming experience, and not every connection or friendship is equipped to accompany us on this journey. Well-meaning friends might offer advice that rushes our grieving process, saying things like "You should be over this by now" or "I don't know why you're still so upset." I recall a friend once telling me after my brother Joel's death that he was better off because the world was becoming a horrible place. I know his heart was in the right place when he said it, but it was a painful comment to hear. Sometimes, even well-intentioned people have their limits when it comes to empathy and understanding.

Our world has changed, and the people we expect to be there for us may not be as available as we hoped. This is a natural part of the grieving process. It's also crucial for us to set boundaries with people as we navigate grief. You don't owe anyone an explanation for your experience. If you feel like talking and there's a listening and understanding ear, that's one thing. However, some individuals may insist that you speak or open up about your grief when you're not ready to. It's essential to prioritize your own comfort and well-being in these situations.

Isolation can become the enemy of grief. Yet, it's entirely natural to want to be alone during this time. As we move through grief and attempt to process our emotions, it can become increasingly difficult to believe that anyone truly understands us. This sense of isolation can be extremely lonely, making you feel like you're the only person on Earth going through what you are. But I promise you, somebody out there gets it. While their experiences might not be identical, they understand the depths of grief. It's a challenge we often face. We need social support and connection to successfully navigate and integrate our loss into the next phase of our lives. However, we tend to look to the familiar, our established networks of friends, peers, workgroups, and social circles.

I've had the privilege of meeting countless incredible people and forming lifelong friendships that would never have happened if not for Joel's death. One such experience is unique to Maine and is called the ***Summit Project***. This nonprofit organization, founded by current and former military members, aims to share the memory and legacy of Maine's fallen soldiers with the public. The project began by asking the families of the fallen to provide a stone that holds significance to the memory of their loved one. Our family chose a stone from our family camp on Silver Lake in Lee. Joel spent countless hours there, making it the perfect choice to honor his memory. These stones were engraved with the name, rank, birth, and death dates of the soldiers, and then they were carried by members of the public, along with family members, on hikes, rucks, marathons, and various other events. Through these outings, I've gotten to know many families of other Maine fallen soldiers. Many of these individuals are now like family to me and my family. Connecting with families who have experienced the loss of a soldier they loved has been a life-changing experience for all of us. During these events, we share not only our loved ones' stories but also our own journeys through grief. We understand each other on a level that is hard, if not impossible, to replicate in any other setting. There is immense validation in the normalization of grief experiences. I've spoken with parents and siblings who have had nearly identical feelings and pathways through their grief journey. Even if we go months or years without seeing some of these individuals, every time we reconnect, it's like picking up where we left off with an old friend—someone who leaves you feeling loved and fulfilled.

There's also the Maine Run for the Fallen organization, which started in 2009. A mile was run for every fallen soldier, and the event aimed to honor Maine's fallen heroes. These events offered Gold Star families the opportunity to connect and share their experiences, while many members of the public participated in the run to show their support.

The Summit Project is just one example of how stepping outside our established social circles can lead to powerful and meaningful connections. ***House in the Woods*** is another such example. This organization has numerous healing qualities, and social connection is certainly one of them. Military members often thrive in a community of like-minded, mission-focused individuals. They live on or near military bases, where their families understand one another, and they have access to various resources provided by the military to ensure soldiers and their families are cared for and prepared for duty.

During combat deployments, military members form incredibly close bonds. They describe their relationships as sisterhood and brotherhood. They endure unimaginable hardships together for months or even years. While they talk about their families back home and miss their loved ones, during deployment, they become each other's family. They experience loss—sometimes the loss of a comrade—and return to their duties the very next day. There is time for ceremony and remembrance on the base, but it's not a space to truly grieve. Combat missions don't allow for the necessary time, space, and support to process a loss as profound as the death of a biological sibling. Those who remain stuck in grief during deployment might even be deemed unfit for service, adding another layer of hardship.

Deployments eventually end, and those who are fortunate return home. However, something has changed. A part of them remains on foreign soil—memories of fallen comrades, survivor's guilt, and the years away from their beloved families. While life has moved forward at home, they feel like outsiders. Families have learned to function without them. Reintegrating into family life is possible, especially with the support of military structures, but it's not always easy. This sense of being an outsider is a common experience among service members, their spouses, and their children.

But what happens when their military service concludes? What occurs when they retire or their enlistment comes to an end? What about the National Guard or part-time service members who return from deployment and are expected to transition back to normal life, family, and careers without the support and normalization of military structure? The answers to these questions are often ambiguous. Veterans may experience confusion, isolation, uncertainty, and fear. Many describe a loss of connection and a deep yearning for the camaraderie they had while serving. I've also spoken with veterans who are stuck in the grief of losing their brothers and sisters in arms. Who better to understand their experiences than other current or former service members?

House in the Woods offers veterans the opportunity to connect, share, and heal in a way that feels organic and unstructured. Veterans attend outdoor events such as week-long hunting or fishing trips, and they begin connecting with one another from day one. There's often someone on the periphery, a lone wolf who is unsure if he wants to join the pack.

Our groups don't discriminate based on age, sex, service branch, or deployment status—everyone is welcome. Over the years, we've witnessed many beautiful stories stemming from these retreat experiences. One story that stands out is that of a Vietnam veteran who attended a bear-hunting retreat. Most attendees were younger, in their 20's to 40's, but this veteran was in his 70's. He shared how he returned home from Vietnam to a nation that hated him. He felt like an outsider. Despite being a successful entrepreneur, married with children, he had always carried a heavy burden. For over 40 years, every day after work, he would take a shower and sob uncontrollably, thinking about his loss and his experiences in Vietnam. As far as he knew, no one, not even his wife, knew about this daily ritual. He had chosen to suffer in isolation, believing that no one could understand or possibly care about what he had gone through. However, after attending one of our retreats a few months before the bear hunt, he experienced a transformation. The other attendees and his Maine guide were Vietnam veterans, and he slowly started opening up to the group. He healed during that week, he said. He no longer felt the need to do it alone, and the daily shower cries had nearly stopped.

This powerful story is just one of many that demonstrate how retreats like **House in the Woods** can have a profound impact on individuals. Retreats offer social connection, guidance, expert intervention, skill-building, and a sense of community. From a counseling perspective, attending a retreat can be equivalent to months of weekly, one-hour counseling sessions. Retreats foster connections and facilitate healing in ways that are difficult, if not impossible, to experience outside of such environments.

While all retreats are not the same, and all losses are unique, I believe that retreats have the potential for transformation. Some retreats may focus on general grief and loss, while others may specialize in specific types of loss, such as the death of a child, divorce, suicide, or betrayal. **Guerrilla Grief Retreats**, for example, provide a safe and healing space for men and women to share their loss experiences and heal. Many of our retreats are nature-based, emphasizing the shared experience of grief as a life force and a means of unlocking our untapped potential. Bearing witness to another's pain and having our own pain witnessed is one of the most genuine and powerful forms of connection.

This book on guerrilla grief isn't solely for veterans and their experiences, but we can learn valuable lessons from some of the toughest and most resilient members of our society. Social communities aren't limited to one or two entities; countless opportunities for meaningful connections exist in our daily lives. Having a close friend who can simply listen is a great place to start. Research even supports the idea that social connection is one of the most powerful factors for predicting longevity. We don't need countless friends and connections, but those of us lucky enough to have one or two close friends who will lend us $100 or help us (though not recommended) bury a body will feel safer and more secure with that support.

Regardless of your loss experience, I encourage you to seek out a community that can understand your journey better than others can. This might take the form of a divorce support group, a child loss group, a suicide survivors' group, or one focused on career loss, among others. These groups don't have to become your entire identity, but more often than not, people find the most growth when they can heal from their own losses and help others who have experienced similar grief.

Now, a bit more about retreat-style healing. I strongly recommend attending a retreat specific to your loss experience. While retreats aren't one-size-fits-all, and due diligence is necessary before committing, I find retreats to be the most potentially transformative of all the interventions we discuss in this book. Here's why:

Imagine attending a four-day retreat where you engage in healing activities for 6-8 hours each day. That alone is arguably equivalent to over half a year of individual, one-hour-per-week counseling sessions. Retreats offer social connections, guidance from experts, skill-building opportunities, and a sense of community. From a counseling perspective, it's like condensing months of therapy into a concentrated timeframe. Retreats facilitate connections and healing that are often challenging to achieve elsewhere.

Of course, not all retreats are created equal, and not all losses are the same. Some retreats focus on general grief and loss, while others concentrate on specific types of loss, such as the death of a child, divorce, suicide, or betrayal. **Guerrilla Grief Retreats**, which I'm passionate about, provide a safe and healing space for men and women to share their loss experiences and embark on a path to healing. Many of our retreats are nature-based, emphasizing the power of shared grief as a source of growth and untapped potential. Bearing witness to each other's pain and having our pain witnessed is a profoundly authentic and transformative experience.

As you explore the concept of guerrilla grief and the role of social connection in healing, remember that your journey is not one you have to navigate alone. Seek out support and communities that resonate with your experiences, and consider the transformative power of retreats. Together, we can learn from the profound impact of human connection in the face of loss and discover how it can be a beacon of hope on the path to healing.

CHAPTER 9 – SPIRITUAL

Hey there! Guess what? You have a spiritual side! Exciting, isn't it? Well, maybe not exactly. But here's the deal - we all have a form of spirituality, whether we fully embrace it or not. As Viktor Frankl, the renowned psychiatrist and Holocaust survivor, once said,

"When we are no longer able to change a situation, we are challenged to change ourselves."

That's not just my opinion, it's something I've come to understand through my personal journey, extensive research, and careful observation. But let's get one thing straight – this isn't about me, it's about you and your fellow men who are navigating the challenging waters of grief. My true goal here is to offer you a glimpse of possibility, a chance to open doors that you may have once closed on your spiritual identity.

A Humorous Nudge Towards Spirituality

Now, I'm not suggesting you rush off to the nearest church, but who knows, it might do you some good! That's my attempt at humor, but on a serious note, within the counseling and grief work communities, we've noticed that individuals who embrace a higher force, being, or even just curiosity about the unknown tend to find a foothold more easily on their grief journey.

Putting Your Spiritual Identity to the Test

So, here's my advice: If you've already got a spiritual identity that's easily accessible, now is the time to put it to the test. It doesn't matter if you're Buddhist, Hindu, Jewish, Muslim, Christian, a follower of the Quaker Oats, a Yogi, or a devoted member of the Church of the Flying Spaghetti Monster, if you've invested a part of your being and life in embracing a particular religious or spiritual journey, grief is an excellent place to put your faith to the test.

Sun Tzu's Principle of Adaptability

Just as Sun Tzu, the ancient Chinese military strategist, famously said,

"In war, the way is to avoid what is strong and to strike at what is weak."

In the **guerrilla warfare of grief**, adaptability is key. Your spiritual side can be that adaptable force, helping you navigate through the emotional battlefield of loss.

The Healthy Act of Questioning Beliefs

Now, I want to emphasize that it's perfectly healthy and natural to question your beliefs, especially in times of grief. This questioning is a critical part of personal growth. I bring this up because I'm aware that some fundamentalist religions condemn any form of curiosity as a sin, threatening eternal damnation and hellfire for those who dare to question. I've been part of this journey myself, where questioning was seen as a fundamental sin.

The Dangers of Cognitive Dissonance

Cognitive dissonance is the discomfort that arises when we hold conflicting beliefs or try to convince ourselves that we feel differently than we do. Many individuals are caught in this trap, especially when it comes to religious beliefs and matters of the heart. Much like a dam holding back water, cognitive dissonance can only contain your doubts and conflicts for so long before they burst out at the most inconvenient times, much like grief itself.

Questioning, Grief, and Loss

Working through and finding what aligns with your belief system, and letting go of the things that no longer work, is also a form of grief and loss. Isn't it fascinating how grief manages to sneak its way into every corner of our lives? But remember, grief isn't the enemy; it's a loving reminder of our shared human experience, offering us opportunities for growth that we might struggle to find otherwise.

As Viktor Frankl wisely noted,

"When we are no longer able to change a situation, we are challenged to change ourselves."

In the face of grief, you may not be able to change the loss you've experienced, but you can certainly change and adapt how you navigate through it. Embracing your spiritual side can be a profound catalyst for that change.

When a person genuinely comes to grips with their spirituality, they're primed for growth. Add a little grief to the mix, and you have a recipe for growth beyond your wildest imagination. So, do you think you have what it takes to delve into your spiritual self? I believe you do, and in fact, you're doing it right now by reading this. Don't stop here, there's an excellent chance that you'll find results you'll come to love. Maybe not immediately, but remember, this journey is a marathon, not a sprint, so dig in and ride it patiently to the top.

I acknowledge that spirituality is a highly diverse and personal aspect of each individual. It's far from uniform, and bringing up the subject often makes people uncomfortable. Spirituality often gets tangled up with religion, myth, or hocus-pocus that feels disconnected from our daily lives. Many have had negative experiences with religion, which can trigger intense, even visceral, emotions.

I'm not here to tell you to "find religion" in your time of loss; quite the opposite. My goal is to share the perspective that we all have a spiritual side, regardless of our affiliations or experiences. As you read this, take a moment to ask yourself what emotions arise when you think about your spirituality. Is it anger? Anger is a common response, especially for those who've faced negative outcomes in places of worship, like churches or synagogues. Strong, negative emotional responses or a complete denial of spirituality can be signs that you're carrying around stuck grief which must be acknowledged and processed as you embark on your journey toward becoming a fulfilled griever.

As I mentioned earlier, I believe that we all have a spiritual side, and nothing illuminates that side quite like a loss or experience of grief. Grief can make us doubt our faith, cause confusion about our belief systems, or reaffirm our faith as unwavering.

It's essential to remember that it's entirely natural, healthy, and even uncomfortable to have questions about your faith and spiritual side, especially in times of loss. My own experiences might shed some light on this matter.

In the story of **House in the Woods**, spirituality and faith play pivotal roles. My father, a devout Christian, exemplified unwavering dedication to what he believed was God's purpose for him. After the untimely passing of my brother, Joel, our family found solace in the belief that we would be reunited with him someday. At Joel's funeral, my father delivered a poignant eulogy, beautifully illustrating Joel's departure from this earthly realm. He envisioned a moment when Joel's burdens lifted, and Jesus welcomed him, saying,

"Well done, my good and faithful servant, your mission on Earth is complete."

This profound narrative, woven in the midst of our deepest grief, provided us with a glimmer of hope and a profound sense of peace.

As my father recounts the genesis of **House in the Woods**, he reminisces about standing in the living room of Joel's church friends in Fort Hood. In a previous chapter on resilience, I shared how God spoke to him, urging him to create a program that would bring military members and their families to Maine, offering them healing amidst the peace and serenity Joel cherished. It's my belief that his unwavering faith served as the bedrock of his resilience, unwaveringly guiding him on this mission. Along the way, we witnessed numerous miracles and inexplicable events, as if divine forces were conspiring to pave the way for us.

Early on, financial constraints posed a substantial challenge. But, like a beacon of hope, a visit from a wealthy retired businessman injected new-found life into our construction project. Despite the completion of the building, financial hurdles persisted. Being a nonprofit, we relied on fund-raising and donations to sustain our retreats, and in two separate years, we faced the daunting prospect of an insurance bill we couldn't afford. Like clockwork, in the nick of time, a check arrived—twice—just as we were teetering on the brink of an insurance lapse.

While a significant portion of our building's cost was generously donated, we still carried a substantial "patience loan" of approximately $1.5 million as a small, growing nonprofit. The prospect of paying off this debt loomed large and threatened to strain our already tight budget. Then, a Christmas miracle unfolded in 202. An anonymous donor stepped forward, offering to clear our entire loan, a staggering $1.5 million. This generous act not only brought immense relief but also allowed us to allocate all our funds towards veteran programming, building a financial reserve, initiating an endowment, and exploring new avenues for growth and impact.

As I share this spiritual journey of **House in the Woods**, my intention isn't to convince you to embrace a particular belief but to encourage you, as I was inspired by my father's example, to contemplate your own spiritual life. Consider how it can fuel your sense of purpose beyond imagination. My father's unwavering faith instilled in him the certainty that God was orchestrating the entire project, providing resources in His time and way. In the face of resistance and doubt, he pressed on. I invite you to reflect on your own spiritual path and how it can ignite your purpose to new heights.

CHAPTER 10 – YOUR NEW BEGINNING

In the throes of fresh grief, the pain is raw and all-consuming. It stings, keeps you awake at night, and makes you feel as though you're on the brink of breaking down. In these initial moments, it can be challenging to discern progress.

Acute grief is the stage that follows immediately after a loss. While there's no fixed timetable for this phase, it can persist for up to six months or even longer. As I mentioned earlier regarding emotional regulation, this stage can be incredibly disorienting. Think of it as akin to a crisis. In a medical crisis, such as a car accident with severe injuries, the primary goal is to rush the individual to a hospital for emergency care. The focus is on stabilizing the person—stopping the bleeding, monitoring vital signs, and ensuring the best possible chances for recovery post-stabilization.

Acute grief can be likened to this scenario. It may not feel like progress is being made, but you can fact-check this. Are you reaching out for the emotional equivalent of "emergency care"? Are you taking the necessary steps to stabilize yourself with the support of others to enhance your long-term prospects? In Cognitive Behavioral Therapy, we often align our feelings and thoughts with discernible facts. In this case, you might not "feel" like what you're doing is effective, but if you're actively working toward stabilization and accepting support from others, you can be confident that you're on the path to recovery and grief integration.

The period following acute grief, known as *"**New Grief**,"* marks the next phase of your grief journey. This stage typically begins around six months after the loss and may extend for a year or more. By this point, you should have established a sense of emotional regulation, and you'll likely start to "feel" that you've made progress.

A word of caution about New Grief - It's the phase when commemorative events start occurring for the first time since the loss. These could include birthdays, anniversaries, holidays, and more. These milestones can often feel like setbacks, as they may trigger memories and intense longing for the person or situation you've lost, evoking feelings of regression. However, it's essential to recognize that they are not true setbacks. Instead, view them as opportunities to gain a deeper understanding of your progress. It's okay to allow yourself to feel the emotions that arise during these times, to sit with the sadness as it comes, but remember not to dwell there longer than necessary. Acknowledge your feelings but keep moving forward on your journey of healing and integration.

As you navigate through new grief you will find with time that things begin to return to a sense of normalcy. While this third timeline phrase of grief may be called several things I will simply refer to it as *"**normal**."* You will, in a sense, feel that life has returned to a degree of normality. Time has given you the opportunity to heal, to process, and to grow. You have embraced a journey that felt impossible at times. You chose to persevere and move forward. This normal is different than any normal you have felt before, you are different. You have embraced pain and uncertainty, you have found strength where you did not know that you had it. As you move forward with life you have now integrated a powerful experience of grief and loss that has transformed you into a more rounded, wiser, and more selfless man.

This new man, however, is not perfect. You are not supposed to be. In fact, through your pain of grief and loss, you have been forged one step closer to the perfection that you alone are on this earth to achieve. Your unique journey offers the ability to reach others in a way that only you can do. You don't have to feel like you have it all together all of the time, that is not a prerequisite for healing and growing from grief and loss. You only have to be honest and genuine with yourself and those that you love and care for. This includes allowing yourself space and forgiveness to heal as you need to, to fall but to get back up, and to know that even the fall is meant to be a part of your experience. As you have read this **Guerrilla Grief Manual** as a practical guide to integrating grief, I hope that you have gained actionable, immediate steps to begin your healing journey. I also implore you to continue to develop your own path forward and embrace the things that truly work to help you heal and grow. Guerrilla grief means just that, you will press on, you will do whatever is required to win the war for your heart.